Tigers

Contents

Big Cats 2
Cubs 6
In the Shade 10
In the River 12
In the Wild 14
Index 16

Written by Pam Rushby

Big Cats

Tigers are big cats.
They are the biggest cats of all.
Tigers are from Asia.

Tigers have stripes.
These stripes hide them in the grass.
Tigers hide there when they hunt.
This tiger is hunting.

Cubs

Baby tigers are called cubs.
These cubs are about two weeks old.
They like to sleep.
They like to play.

These cubs are about
three months old.
They will learn about hunting.
They will learn about staying safe.
Then, they will leave home.

In the Shade

These tigers lie about in the shade.
They stay cool there.

In the River

These tigers swim in the river.
Tigers like to swim.
They drink there.
They stay cool there.

In the Wild

Now, there are few wild tigers.
Now, there are only about 3,500.
Parks like these protect tigers.
These tigers are safe there.

Index

cats 2
cubs 6, 8
grass 4
parks 14
river 12
stripes 4